FOR THIS ALONE

& OTHER POEMS

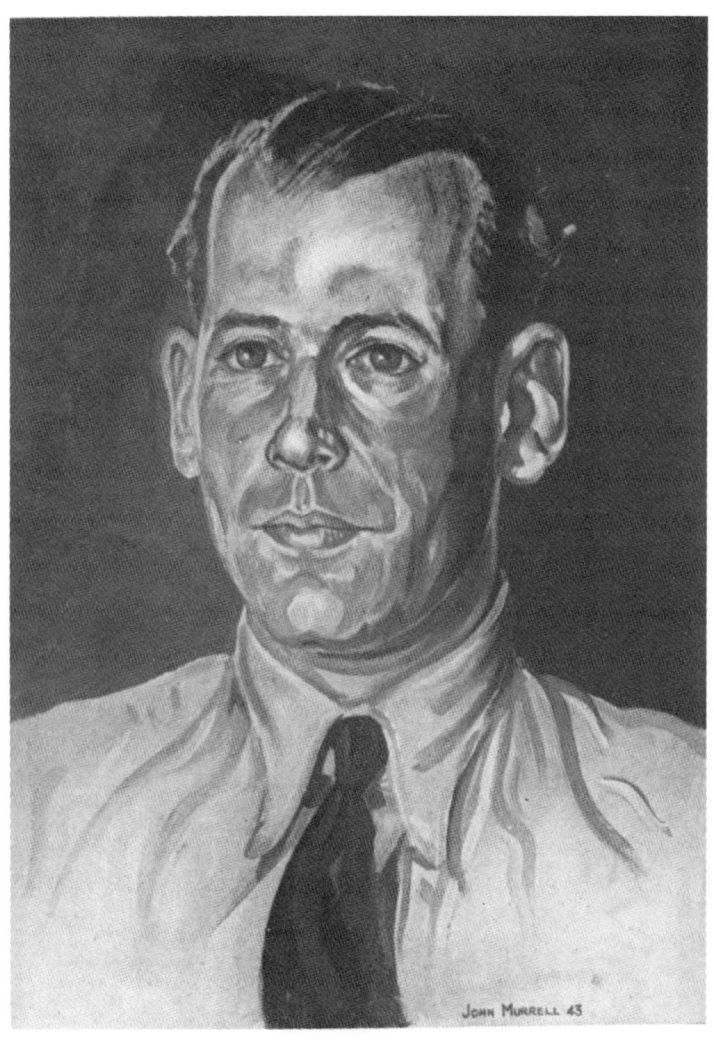

W/O R. P. L. Mogg
From a painting made in Stalag 357, Germany,
by John Murrell, 1943.

FOR THIS ALONE

& OTHER POEMS

BY

R. P. L. MOGG

UNIFORM
PRESS

This edition published in 2014 by Uniform Press, an imprint of Unicorn Press Ltd.

66 Charlotte Street
London
W1T 4QE
www.unicornpress.org

978-1-910065-20-4

5 4 3 2 1

Printed in India by Imprint Digital
Designed by Lucy Duckworth

For This Alone & Other Poems originally published in 1944 by Basil Blackwell, Oxford and dedicated to James A. G. Deans, Sergeant Pilot, R.A.F.
Time to Stand and Stare originally published in 1945 by Basil Blackwell, Oxford and dedicated to Peter Thomas:

> All prisoners of war eventually find something with which to occupy their minds. They have to; it is the only way to keep sane. Work is the great anodyne.
> Peter is one of the busiest prisoners I know. His activities range from studying and coaching law; to acting in, producing and advising on the production of plays. He also finds time to be the mainspring of the Debating Society and the President of the Welsh Society. In spite of all this activity he has always managed to lend a kindly and, what is more important, a critical ear to the verse which arises from my attempts to keep myself busy.
> Thank you, Peter.

CONTENTS

All of the poems in this collection were written in German prisoner of war camps. They were written in moods of every kind, and moods take up a large part of the non-working prisoner's existence.

Moods or feelings that at home would pass unnoticed or would not even exist, bulk large here. The prisoner secures a new set of values, and more important, he achieves *detachment*.

He stands alone in a world, of his own; the clangour of the battle all around him is muted by his surroundings and his immediate necessities. He belongs to the world but he is not part of it. To preserve himself he has to forget the squalor and unhappiness around him and learn how to slip away to the enchanted country of the mind.

It is natural, then, that his thoughts and values are in some respects different from those of people at home. It is natural that some things should take on what might appear to be a false value, and that every well-loved ugly duckling, laved in the beauty of imagination and the passage of the years, becomes a golden swan. This is so; but the prisoner has the advantage of *knowing* that it is so, and that his present values are liable to be only temporary ones.

All the same, the mark and habits of these years of imprisonment will not fade quickly; and the prisoner will return home to the things he has left, and take of them with a new awareness. His appreciation will be deepened, broadened and simplified.

Take a simple thing like the night for instance. For two years many of us were locked in shuttered rooms at night. We never had a full glimpse of the night sky, but only odd little corners of it. It seemed as if part of our life was missing.

Raiding had already made the night the friend of many of us.

Time and again we had slipped out of the danger of searchlights into the friendly covering of the jungle of darkness. Danger lived there too, but we felt more comfortable in the night's friendly clasp.

Then for two years the night sky was denied to us.

Lately we have been able to go out at night and our friendship with the unlimited regions of darkness has become stronger than ever before. We have gone out with a new awareness, to greet our former companions, the clouds and the stars.

Most prisoners become cynical, but not disillusioned. Their cynicism is touched with humour, although sometimes it is a bitter humour.

As for the future, they know that some disenchantment is in store for them. It is bound to be. But they have Hope, and that is the one thing that cannot be taken from the prisoner. It is hope that has sustained him in the weary, useless, circle of the years.

And now the hope of the future is before them. New and greater adventures are ahead when they set out to help rebuild, from the wreckage that they have helped to make, a new and greater inheritance based on the values learned in adversity.

   R. P. L. Mogg
    R.A.F.
    Camp 357, Germany, 1944

Being a journalist by profession, Sgt. R. P. L. Mogg was not new to the art of writing but this collection of poems represented a new venture. He left the newspaper world to join the R.A.F. and his experiences in flying provided the subject matter for his poems. Shot down over Germany and taken a prisoner in the early part of the war he discovered that he had a considerable amount of time to indulge in literary diversions. These poems written during this period are the product of an airman's mind but their appeal will be universal.

It is possible that he may be accused of being morbid, but the dividing line between operational flying and Death is of a very nebulous character.

'Heldentod' was set to music by another Prisoner-of-War Sgt. H. W. Bradley as it was considered that together they would constitute excellent broadcasting material.

By the clever use of vivid illustration Sgt. J. W. Lambert has put Sgt. Mogg's words into picture form.

Altogether this book represents many hours of enjoyable work executed to while away what might have been dull moments in a Prisoner-of-War Camp.

CREW ROOM

Bright lights,
chatter of voices,
bulky figures in flying clothes.
And, over all
the sharp conglomerate smell
of aircraft dope,
and oil,
and petrol.

Men
playing draughts:
planning routes on charts,
or packing bags.
But mainly,
talking.

Dispersal lorries,
noise crescendo,
dying, dying.
Then, empty room and
bright lit silence.
But always,
the tart, nostalgic smell
of aircraft dope,
and oil,
and petrol.

CAPTIVE AIRMEN

For these the bloodless agony of the soul.
The hard unending days:
The unfilled minutes.
The round and round, within the wire,
Till body, brain and life itself
Go round,
And round, and round,
Encompassed by omnipotent, unfeeling wire.

Oh, what bright hopes have burned
Within these hearts
Which once beat quick with high endeavour.
Oh, what bright hopes,
What dreams.
Now these must walk upon
The bitter treadmill of captivity;
And live each laggard second
To its fullest ends
Of uselessness.

These who once rode the storm
And quelled the trembling earth;
Who crushed proud cities,
And tore the sky asunder with their might;
These who once knew companionship
With birds and clouds and stars;
Who spread Youth's oriflamme in the sky,
Earthbound, rotate within the wire.

And, these are they
Who from this agony will surmount
With greater strength the loftier heights;
They wait, held constant
By their thoughts of Home,
And dream new dreams
Of hope.

On Week-end Leave

Day filled a room with early light.
It touched a table ... all your things were there.
It lay across the bed and lit your hair.
Your teeth flashed bright as in the rosy stream
You stirred and smiled, and murmured in a dream
Before you too awoke and banished Night.

RAID

I. TAKE OFF
The bruised air
Sweeps turbulent behind.
Airscrews grasping
The night haze,
The bombers leap into the sky.
They leave the air
Trembling, pulsating
With the mutter of their Power.

Motors roar
Their trumpet note
Across the long blue reaches
Of the sky.
Night's thick ocean
Closes round
And clasps the bombers
In its solitude.

Night-smudged
Earth slips away,
Falling, falling, fading
To a black sea of nothing.

Held in the womb of Night.
This is magnificence
Beyond all human comprehension.
This is Splendour
Greater than death.
Sirens
Herald the bombers' march
Across the trembling continent.

II. THE SIREN

The dark jungle of houses
Presses up on either side.
All is quiet.
So quiet the pavement rings
To footsteps,
And the noise echoes back
From the dark-faced houses.
There are no street lights.
No lights anywhere.
The houses seem to tower up endlessly;
Yet their tops
Make a frame for the stars.

The siren
Shrieks,
Wails.
Giving birth to its urgent
Presage of danger.
Noise bursts swelling upwards,
Gigantic bubbles of sound.
Human life
Draws a great breath of fear.
The inanimate stands
In doomed expectation.

In a shop doorway,
Unheeding,
A man and woman entwine;
Locked in the obscene momentum
Of creation.
Conception,

When the foot of death
Makes the city tremble.

O poor humanity.
Little white worms
Crawling under the flat,
Downpressing stone of Ignorance.
Knowing little
But lust and fear,
Hunger and pain.
Fearing the ultimate anonymity
Of the oblivion of Death.
Seeking comfort
In some doctrine of immortality.

O fat little man
Running to the shelter,
Do you consider yourself
A fit subject for
Immortality?
Should you be preserved
Thus,
With the fear-sweat running
Down your white face,
And your bowels liquified?
Should you march thus
Down the ages,

The symbol of our time?
Why not?
You *are* the symbol.
You are not Christ crucified,

An elegant version
Of sacrifice for Ideals.

You are the dumb animal
Bound for the slaughter,
And fearful
At the stink of blood.
You are the worse than nothing,
Because you are in the mould of something
That might be
Inconceivably greater.
There is a splendid uselessness
About your immolation
That cannot be hidden
With brave words.

You are the doomed cattle.
Keep your thoughts downward,
Little Man.
It is dangerous to think too high.

III. THE BOMBERS COME
The bombers
Tread the night sky;
Marching down
The star filled ways.
Thunder of engines
Filling the air before them:
Deep-throated heralds,
Crying,
'We are coming.
We are coming.

Death!'

O poor Humanity,
Get down into the earth:
Away from the night:
Away from the stars.

Raise not your thoughts
To the skies
Humanity,
For death and loveliness
Live there.

Press your eyes downwards.
Keep your thoughts
Earthbound.
Lift not your thoughts or Ideals
Among the great clean concourse
Of the heights,
For there dwell things
Beyond your narrow comprehension.

Only the immediate interests you.
Only the futile crawl
That you miscall living.
Get down into your holes,
Humanity.

IV. BOMBS FROM ABOVE
From above,
Bombs
Seem to burst

Like bright flowers.
Thundering blossoms
In the night.

Incendiaries shine,
Bright daisy-chains beneath.
Fires grow;
Flower beds of flame,
In the lawn of night.

V. IN THE SHELTER
Foetid reek
Grips the throat.
There is a smell of fear.
Conversation, brittle;
Words crack through
The ice of terror.
The place is filled
With what the papers like to call
A 'cross section of our life.'
Child cries:
Someone cracks a joke:
Laughter, drowned
In the rumble of bombs bursting.
There is a nauseous
But pathetic gallantry
About this den.

VI. ALL CLEAR
The horror filled night
Dies to the unhappy hubbub
Of its aftermath.

Dawn creeps timidly
Through the murk of smoke and flame.
Humanity leaves its holes
And defaces the bright morning.

Business as usual.
The elemental moment is passed:
Humanity comes back to its narrow ways.
Its people walk the treadmill
Of existence.

So many burning thoughts
Have been obliterated.
So many lives that had no meaning
Have ceased to be.
The communal grave
Has folded them all
Into the Earth's cool maw.
Their petty strugglings smoothed out,
They are as if they had never been.

VII. Child Killed in Raid
'Gentle Jesus, meek and mild,
Look upon this little child. . .'
O, I have seen dead children
Smiling gently; wearing
The ethereal garment
That makes one liken them
To angels.
And there has been
A delicate mask of beauty
All about them.

But there is nothing beautiful in this.
These grotesque, twisted limbs,
These splintered fingers:
Bloodied entrails, looped
On the dark pavement:
And dead, grey face
Still fixed with horror.
And eyes ...
Eyes like dead fishes' eyes,
Unblinking, fixed.

I suppose
This grotesque parody
Of sacrifice will be
Commemorated with some splendid words
And tall stone pillars.

EPILOGUE
That speck of almost nothing,
The world,
Reels uneasily through
The great seas of space.
The Little Man continues
His futile reproduction;
Attaining little, but
A few thin scratches on the face of Time;
The dust, and nothing.
                    Amen.

Nightmare

The black walls of night press around
With invisible power.
The hands of the Darkness reach out
With their moth-wing touch.
There is silence. *Black* silence.
Be still!
Don't breathe. Or they'll hear you,
The bat-winged, long-toothed ones
That habit the Night.

They creep through the darkness
Pressing in close,
With their silent cries,
And their foetid breath,
And their frog-like touch.

They suck blood from the heart,
And thoughts from the brain.
Foul venomous creatures.
They dance their wild rout
On a floor made of skulls.
Human skin on their drums.
Human bones for their sticks.

They live in the darkness
Never quite taking shape.
They hang in the trees,
In the shadows they lurk.
All you may see
Is the flash of their teeth,
Their long yellow teeth.
The bat-winged horrors that live in the night.

Never Keep a Lady Waiting

Patricia Mary's very sweet,
From her jet black head
To her tiny feet
And Patricia Mary's waiting.

She wasn't here when war began
She had to wait to meet THE MAN.
But he keeps Patricia waiting.

Patricia Mary looks down the street
She stamps her tiny
Imperious feet
She doesn't like this waiting.

Patricia sheds a sweet shy tear
And looks again
In hope he's near
Patricia Mary's waiting.

Please don't cry, Patricia, Dear.
The naughty man will soon be here
Who keeps Patricia waiting.

*Written for Patricia Jackson (née Hancock),
daughter of Warrant Officer R. C. S. 'Hank'
Hancock, a fellow 'Kriegie' comrade in the
Stalag Luft Administration Offices.*

WIVES

Anxious
we tell the leaden minutes.
Hoping, fearing.
Not for us the burning moments
of conflict.
Or the knowledge
of our destructive task accomplished.
We cannot share in these
or things like these.
We wait.

For us...
At best, brief happiness.
For every welcome
a farewell.
Until the last.
For us the rack
of inert waiting.
Every nerve a point of flame,
watching tense,
the clock hands
make their laggard passage.
Forgetful for a moment,
making dreams.
Waiting...
Knowing...
Dreading...

BEYOND THE WIRE

A dying sun has set the western world afire,
And coloured all the trees,
Where a fragrant little breeze
That blows from England breathes
Lightly among the murmuring trees.
And the universe is lit with fire.
But that's *beyond* the wire.

TIGER TRUTH

Softly silent, the Tiger Truth
Steals through the jungle of the mind.
Swiftly, sure, he springs to slay
The loose fat thoughts,
That are the kin of emptiness and lies.
Stupidity and half truths
Are his prey.

Sinuous the silent Tiger slinks
Through the rancid rottenness
Of thoughts half dead;
Thoughts dead and rotten.
Softly, softly the Tiger treads,
Seeking the WHY.

LULLABY, 1940

Lullaby, my Sweeting,
The bombers won't hurt you;
But when you grow up
The Income Tax will.
Oh, won't it be jolly
To pay for men's folly;
And when you grow old
To be paying it still.

Sleep tight, my Sweeting,
Safe in the shelter;
And when you grow up
In a war you can fight.
Now won't it be thrilling
To join in the killing
With deadlier bombs
Than are falling tonight.

HUNGER

Hunger shines in men's faces,
Liquid, bright,
A grim radiance,
An ethereal pallor
As if the spirit
Had burned away
The grossness of the flesh.

Thoughts glow
With hunger,
White skeletons of truth
Consume the mind.

In hungry men's eyes
There is no lustre.
Their gaze is hollow,
Fixed
On an uttermost beyond.
They inhabit the earth
But are not of it.
They have no actuality.
They are gaunt links
Between life and Nothingness.

As Hunger's sharp knives
Slough the flesh,
Limbs will not do the brain's bidding.
The body floats in a liquid emptiness,
Where the past ceases:
Where there is no present
Except a void

And the future does not exist.
These stumbling caricatures of men
Have no existence but in the mind
Which burns
Until the end
With terrifying clarity.

Hunger clothes men
In a glowing mask
Of remote glory.
There is a terrible loveliness about them,
Shining bridegrooms
Awaiting the strange finality of death.

PRISONER GONE MAD

His dead eyes look beyond the wire;
His ears hear things we cannot hear;
His soul has burned out all its fire;
He knows of only one thing, FEAR.
Fear all powerful: Fear chilling.
Strange, silent Fear, that rots the heart:
Fear like a foul white slug that clots
All thought, and ravages apart
Each nerve, and wreathes the mind in knots.
Fear unknowable: Fear Killing.

'THINGS'LL BE ALRIGHT'

When I can walk the Dwuns again
Zparklen, vresh wi Zummer rain,
And watch the clouds a'zailen high,
Like gurt, vat dragons, in the sky;
And peaceful, I can zet avore
A creeper-twined and zun-warmed door,
And greet the maidens when they come
To zay they'm glad to zee I hwome:
When I can veel the kiss of rain
And zee ponds formen in the lane,
Wi trees above all drippen wet;
Or zet in shade in Zummer het:
When dru the woods comes now and then
The chipperen of the cutty wren:
When idle I can take my ease,
Wi zider and Blue Vinny cheese:
When I zee zunshine in the glade,
Or violets zhy as any maid,
And vuzz a bloomen gold and vair,
Or smell the springtime in the air:
When I can zee the year grow old
And woods alive wi brown and gold:
When I can zee you walken nigh
And catch the zmile that's in your eye:
When winds come raoren from zee,
When cups are clatteren vor tea,
And your vaice is a callen me;
Then, things'll be alright wi me.

In Memory of a conversation held with Pte. . . .
of the Dorset Regt. Spring, 1944, Germany.

Dreams …
Thoughts slip mistily away
Down the steep cool slopes
Of dying consciousness
To Sleep's miasmal caves.

A white road
Lifts itself brightly
Over the hills.
Stone walls … there's no wire here:
Lichened stones border
The road.

The hills soar up
In green joyfulness.
Trees murmur
With the accent
Of scent-laden breezes,
The grasses talk
In a tumult of whisperings
And birds sing
With the bursting heart of freedom.

Awakening
Morning's bright hands
Strip the shadowed
Fantasy of dreams;
Thoughts become
Immediate.
The iron bonds
Tighten on the soul.
The unchanged, ever changing

Pageant of misery
Begins its hollow walk.

Here there is no greenness,
Only the hard shadow
And the dust
And squalor.
Barbed wire cuts across the eyes
Like an ugly wound;
It presses on the sight
And burns
Into the mind.

Here are the dead things.
Here is hope putrified.
Here mummified ideals.
And Youth …
Ah, Youth died long ago.
Here is the haven
Of lost hopes,
The graveyard of ideals.

Soldier Song, 1944

O praise the stalwart miner
Who toils beneath the ground.
For he is worth six quid a week
And I am worth a pound.

For my few shillings daily
I have to work and fight.
But my shift starts at morning,
And it doesn't end at night.

I hold the shattered parapet.
I live down in the mud.
I know the sound and reek of death:
I know the sight of blood.

The thumping of the mortars,
The chatter of the guns,
Obliterating from my mind
I was a civvy once.

I do not fight for glory.
For pay, I do not fight.
I fight for one or two ideals
That I believe are right.

I fight in a great company,
A fellowship, that may
Not stab its comrades in the back
Because they get more pay.

SANDMAN

Along the golden aftermath of day
He comes with tireless step, an old grey man.
With noiseless tread, he makes his gentle way;
And every home he knows. Through every land
He goes, and carries in his kindly hand
A bulging bag of magic sleepy sand.

Among the children in their carefree play
Of make believe, his soothing trade he plies,
His blessing covers all… the sad, the gay;
The foolish; poor; the clever and the wise.
Heads droop and stubborn hands rub sleepy eyes.
Deftly the tender bonds of sleep he ties.

And then, he makes his quiet way
Along the fringe of passing day.

To Marjorie

I wouldn't talk of love,
Remember?
I said it was a word too trite,
too common with the bourgeoisie
to name the delicate consuming power
that flamed through blood,
through thoughts,
through life.
But you seemed unimpressed.
And when I said
that I would pluck the stars
down from their velvet bed
to place about your slender throat,
you laughed,
in that sad way
I loved so much,
and stopped my boasting
with your lips.
Perhaps you knew;
perhaps you read,
the bitter years to come.

FIGHTERS AT DAWN

Swung high
Above the terraced loveliness
Of clouds:
Poised
In the high arched
Vault of blue emptiness
They ride,
Swift minions
Of the Gods of War
And children of the storms:
Bowered in the
Storm God's cradle
For his playthings.
Small black cruciforms
In the red light
Of early morning.

Their shadows chase
Beneath them
Across the fields of chrysolite.
Across cloud hills and valleys
In the blood–light
Of the morning's birth.

The clouds,
Soaring, rising,
Caress these
Their strange new children.
All the sleek beauty
Of the air is theirs.

Out of the red sun
More black shapes
Streak through the
Early morning quiet,
Whirling aside
The dancing whisps
And wraiths of cloud.

Down!
Out of the sun
They come.
Fire points flicker
On wings.
Tracer whirls.

One slips by
In front.
A moment. . .
Rigid across the sights
Stands sharp.

Eight Brownings
Scar the bright morning
With thin lines
Of death.
Flame-limned he turns,
Held for a moment
Almost stationary,
Before he spins,
Twisting,
Flaming,
Down.

Down.
Deep into the white
Cool mysteries
Beneath.

Across the blue early day
They ride.
Sun glints on wings
And perspex,
Like bright–swords–flash.

Only Death's smoke pennant
Curling across the sky
Marks the passage of one
Who knows
The bright awareness of the day
No longer.
Yet *knows*
At last …

OIL WREATH

Across the bright arc of the sky
You spun,
Clasped in the meteor's heart,
Into the sea.
A small spurt of white foam,
As the seas reached out to draw you in,
And you had passed
Beyond us.

We who were left above,
Looked down.
Upon the sea
There spread
A dark, green wreath of oil,
Flowered with great white bubbles,
Bursting from below,
And spreading, spreading.

We never saw you any more,
But we remembered,
Not only your laugh,
And your carefree ways,
But the oil wreath
Circled on the sea.

Prison Midnight

To-day creeps imperceptibly
Into tomorrow
And then becomes a day that was.
All days know their short journey,
Their brief flowering,
And then are memories –
Except days in prison.
These have no beginning,
No ending,
No life.

Days burn clear;
Days are dull.
For some they trace their kaleidoscopic pattern.
Weaving the bright wefts of joy
With the sombre warp of sadness.

Always the future
Marches omnipresent
To the present;
To fade
In a welter of minutes and seconds.

But for us
Days are faceless ghosts
That march remorselessly along
A never ending road of pain,
Through the half-lit tragedy
Of unfulfilment.

Here
There are no burning moments;
No days to be remembered.
Days are just things
To be ticked off on a calendar;
Each tick marking a step
Nearer to an end
That cannot be seen.

Stalag 357,
Germany

HELDENTOD

I
The places where the bullets hit
burn warm.
There is no pain.
Only a gentle ebb of life.

And death,
unheeded in the whirl of combat
in the heights,
treads gently close
in this green English field.

Clouding the bird calls
and the hum of insect
in a cloying mist of weakness.

As life drips out its warm bright drops,
the mind
eager in its last few moments
before oblivion
wipes it clean,
speeds fast.
And quickly spans the gulf of years.

II
Again,
the broad green Polish plain,
slashed by sombre slow-winding rivers,
map-like slips
beneath my wings.

Secure in cold clean heights,
watching doomed towns
stretch their fiery fingers
of bloody agony
at the red sky.

III
Again,
the black bombs drop;
hurtling along the airy columns.
Dwindling. Pin points
shooting along the ground.
Dark seeds of death
among the houses.
Blossoming
in terrible fertility
to flowers of flame and smoke
and dust.

IV
Screamers on…
Stick forward…
Ground
races up.

The small black dots
of men
swim
in the sights.

Muscles tensing.
Quickened heart beat.

A slight pressure...
The guns
hurl whirling tracer
into yielding flesh
and splintering bone.
Each gun
hammers death
nine hundred times a minute.

And I,
happy in the lust to kill,
yet fearful.
Fearing,
I know not what.

V
I think...
bright rods of pain
cloud the swift cinema of the mind.
But pain flows out with life
and weakness brings its gentles anodyne.
Crystal clear
the mind
flicks on.

No time
for thoughts of peace
or home, or gentleness.
Caught in this sharp surge of war,
only war
can hold the flickering thought.

VI
The weakness grows,
stealing along the channels of the heart.
The mind grows quiet.
A few brief heartbeats
left to sum the balance of my life.

This death.
This gentle cradled death.
Is but a price
too gladly paid.
A ransom for the quivering ecstasy
of Flight.
For soul exalting moments
in the sky,
when I have known a harmony
with lofty clouds
and endless, endless space.
And, having known these high delights
I welcome Death.
Unscarred by Age,
this forfeit life
may help me up
to join
the brighter company of the stars.

Gladly then
I die.

FOR THIS ALONE

Was it for this alone
We left the darkness of the womb,
the laughing childhood days?
To go,
but children still
into the lofty places of the Gods.

To play
among the towered cumulus,
and flirt
along the pillared ramparts of the storm.
To watch great clouds
flower in ever-changing shapes.

And see
black crossed, sharp silhouettes
across our sights,
spin
flaming
down.

And then
to know the same fleet death.
The sweet sharp agony.
The searing change
from eager life
back to the shadowed mystery of Oblivion.

Germany, August 1942

NIGHT BOMBERS

Frightening the dusky night our motors roar.
Beneath, the startled earth slides back.
On either hand the cloudy columns soar.
Among the reeling stars we make our track.
We are the War God's eagles.
Two-fifties,
Five-hundreds,
Thousand-pounders,
Four-thousands.

Around, the sullen dark is shot with light,
the whirling, flaming lines of death
reach up, to bar our black-winged eagles flight,
and fan us with their fiery breath.
We are the War God's hammer
Bombs selected…
Running up now…
Left a little…
Bombs Gone.

WAR'S END

You who have dared the holocaust:
You who have cleared the sky:
You who have held the shattered line:
You who have learned to die:
You who have swept the oceans:
You who made cities burn:
You who have been Death's right hand:
To what do you return?

It's hard tack and skilly, my lad,
And poverty for your lot;
A hero you were a week ago,
Now nobody cares a jot.

Requiem for Dead Airmen

In God's blue fields their glory flowered,
burned brightly, then was quenched.
High in the rain-washed spaces they
knew the swift, sharp hour of youth.
And, eager, went
into the long cool vale of death.
Hopes unfulfilled.
Hope realized.
Dreams ended.
Sleep
Begun.